Tools and Wheels

Venice Shone

ORCHARD BOOKS

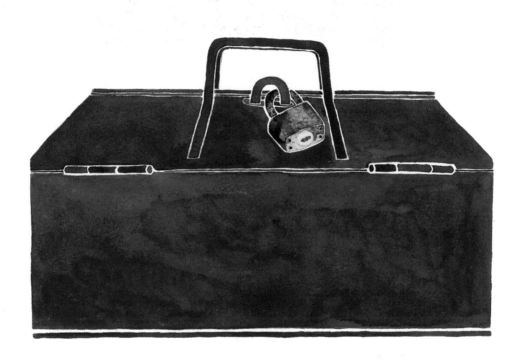

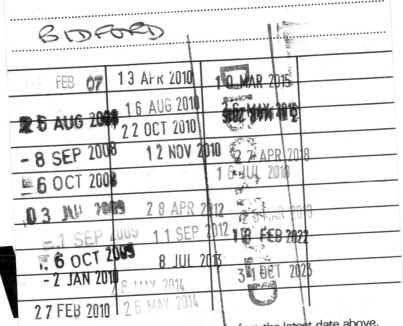

For Edward and Oliver

ORCHARD BOOKS
96 Leonard Street, London EC2A 4XD
Orchard Books Australia
Unit 31/56 O'Riordan Street, Alexandria, NSW 2015
ISBN 1 84121 672 0
Originally published in Great Britain in two separate books,
TOOLS and WHEELS in 1990
This edition first published in 2001
© Venice Shone 1990
The rights of Venice Shone to be identified as the author and
illustrator of this work have been asserted by her in accordance
with the Copyright, Designs and Patents Act, 1988.
A CIP catalogue record for this book is available
from the British Library.
1 3 5 7 9 10 8 6 4 2
Printed in Belgium

Tools

There are lots of different tools people use when they are working. There are tools for cutting, joining, measuring, painting, decorating and gardening. There are even tools for clearing up when all the work is finished!

Remember that many of the tools are heavy and sharp and should only be touched by grown-ups.

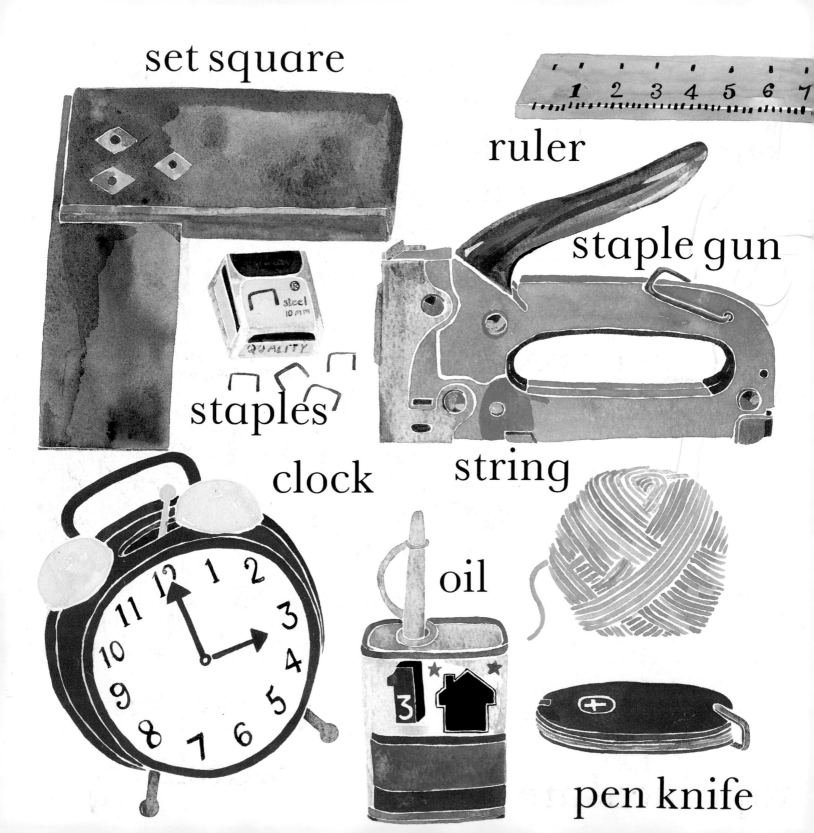

set square

ruler

staple gun

staples

string

clock

oil

pen knife

pencil

bulldog
clip

pad
of paper

**TOOL
book**

padlock

2.0 m

watch

tape measure   key

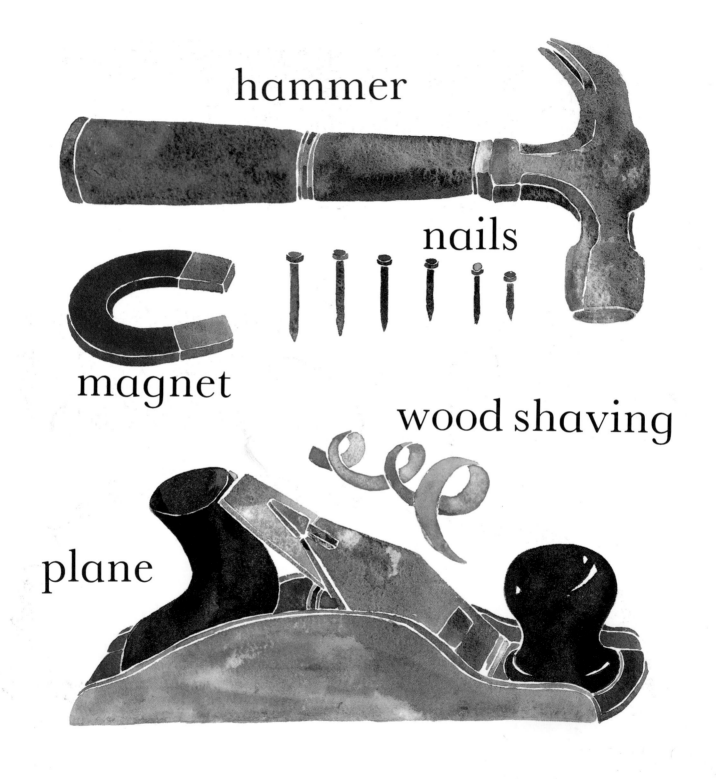

hammer

nails

magnet

wood shaving

plane

saws

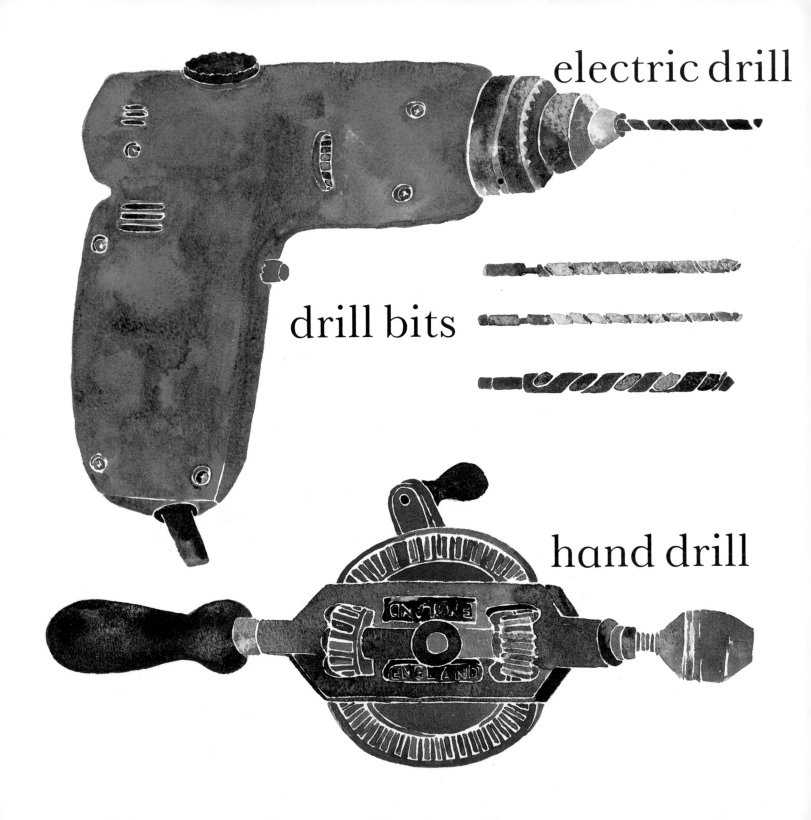

electric drill

drill bits

hand drill

screwdrivers

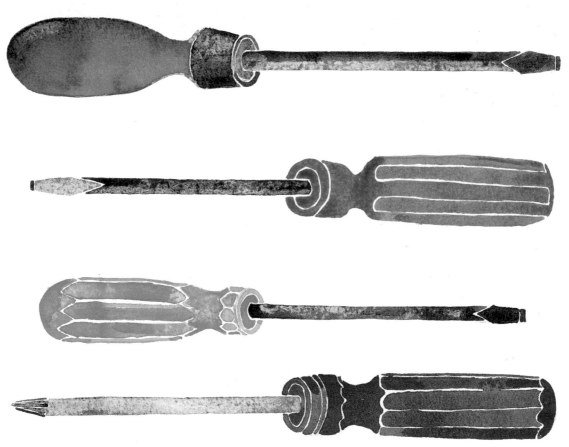

screws

broom

spade

fork

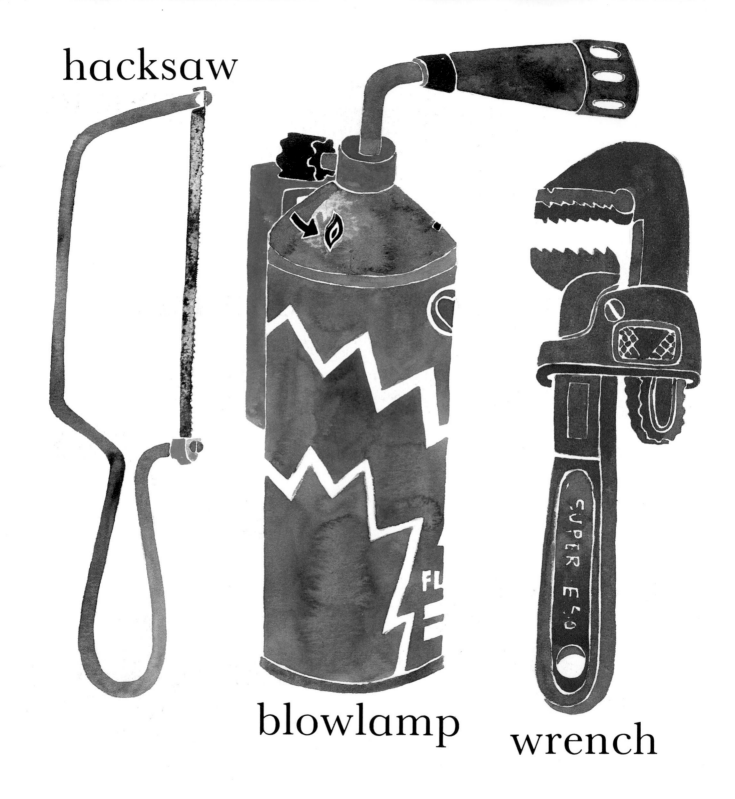

hacksaw

blowlamp

wrench

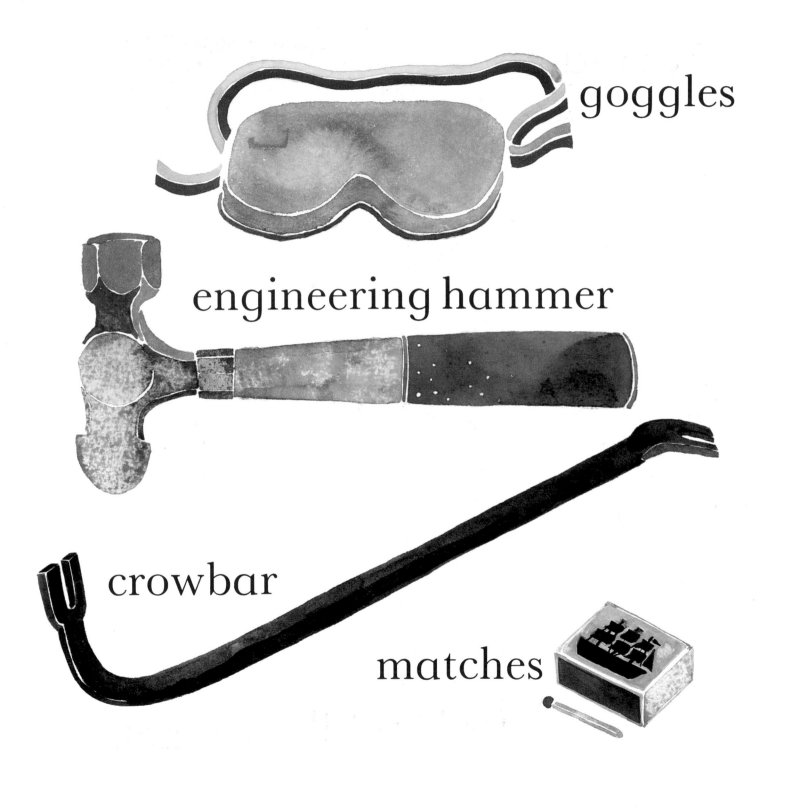

goggles

engineering hammer

crowbar

matches

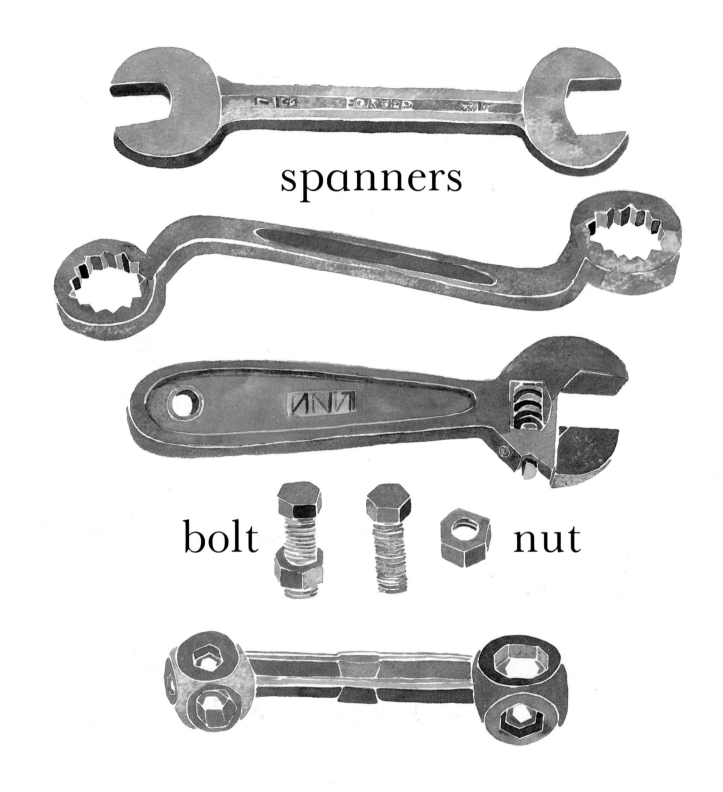

spanners

bolt

nut

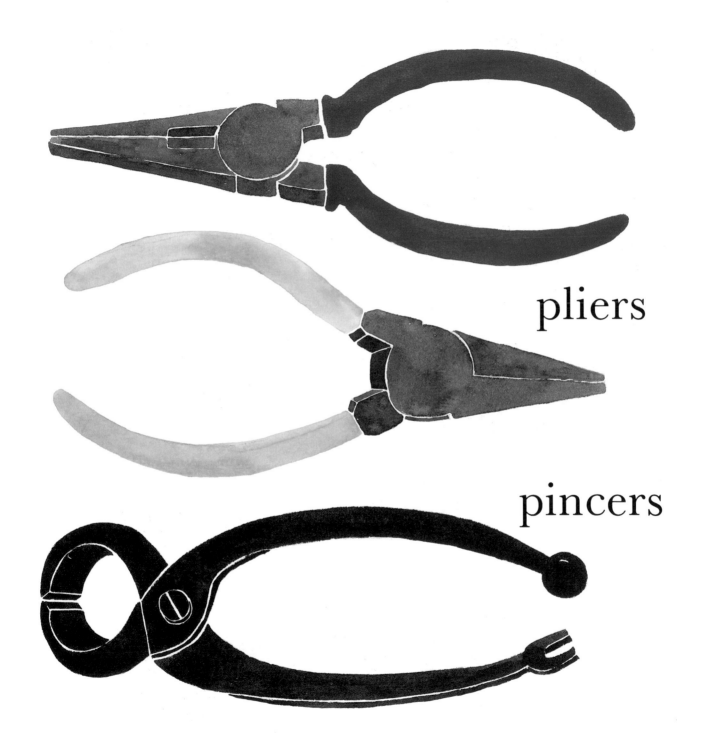

pliers

pincers

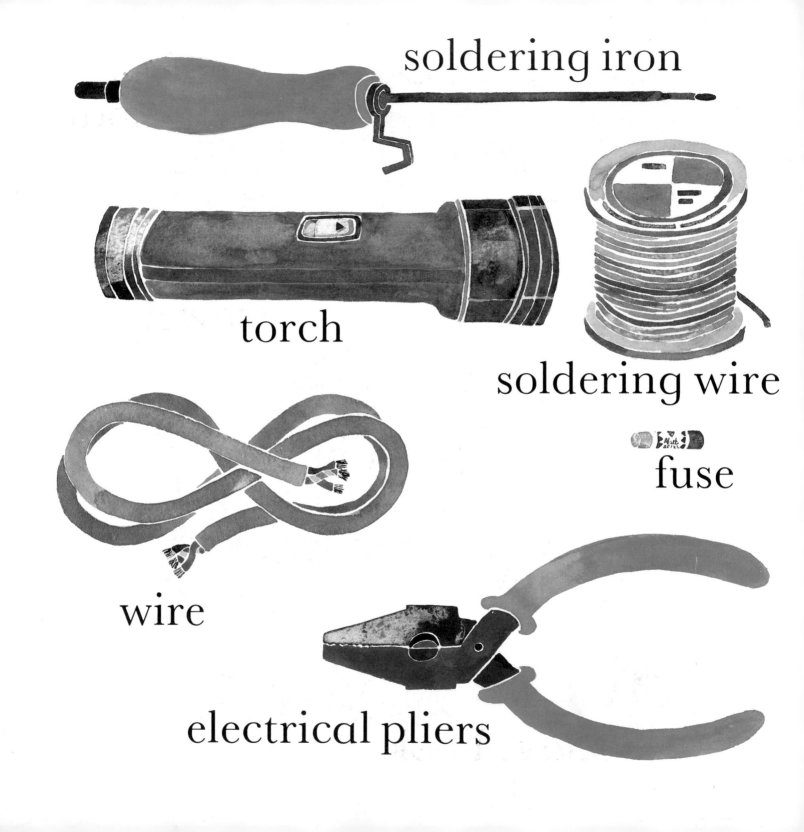

soldering iron

torch

soldering wire

fuse

wire

electrical pliers

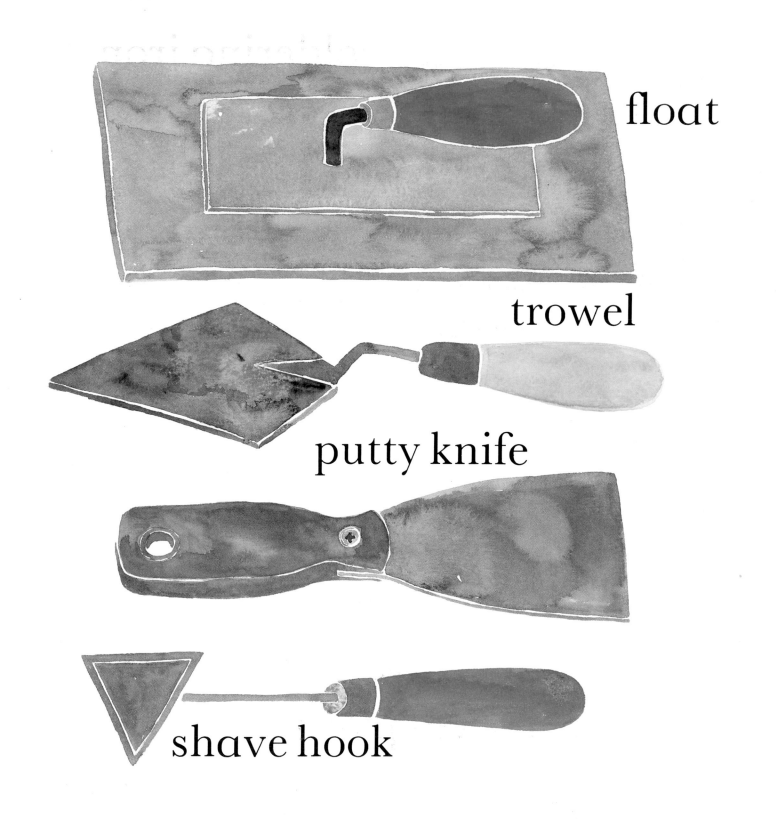

float

trowel

putty knife

shave hook

paintbrush

can of paint

wallpaper brush

cutting knife

wallpaper paste

scissors

ladder

bucket

dustpan
and brush

funnel

glove

white spirit

paint

radio

mug
of tea

first aid
kit

Wheels

Wheels come in all different sizes and on all sorts of vehicles: cars, bicycles, prams - even on shopping trolleys! There are wheels on toys and wheels on rollerskates, as well as wheels on boats and on caravans.

Which sort of wheels are your favourite?

pram

roller skates

tricycle

skateboard

bicycle

St Raphael
GiTANE
CAMPAGNOLO

motorbike

racing car

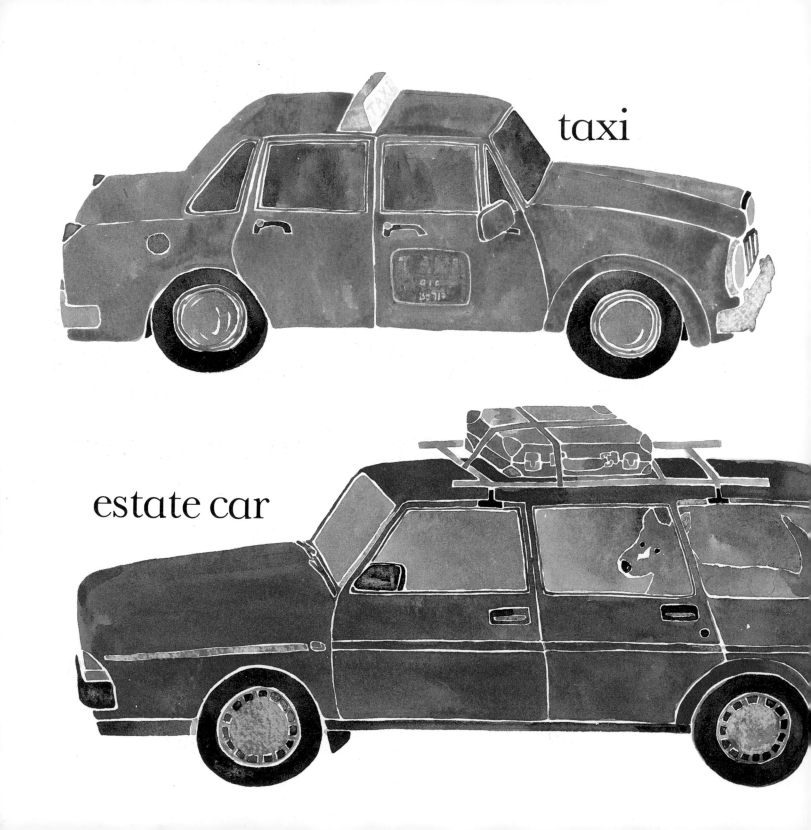

taxi

estate car

wedding car

learner-driver
car

DRIVING
SCHOOL

School

school bus

Bus

coach

BREAD
AND CAKES

baker's van

removal van

laundry van

florist's van

police car

ambulance

fire engine

dump truck

wheelbarrow

cement mixer

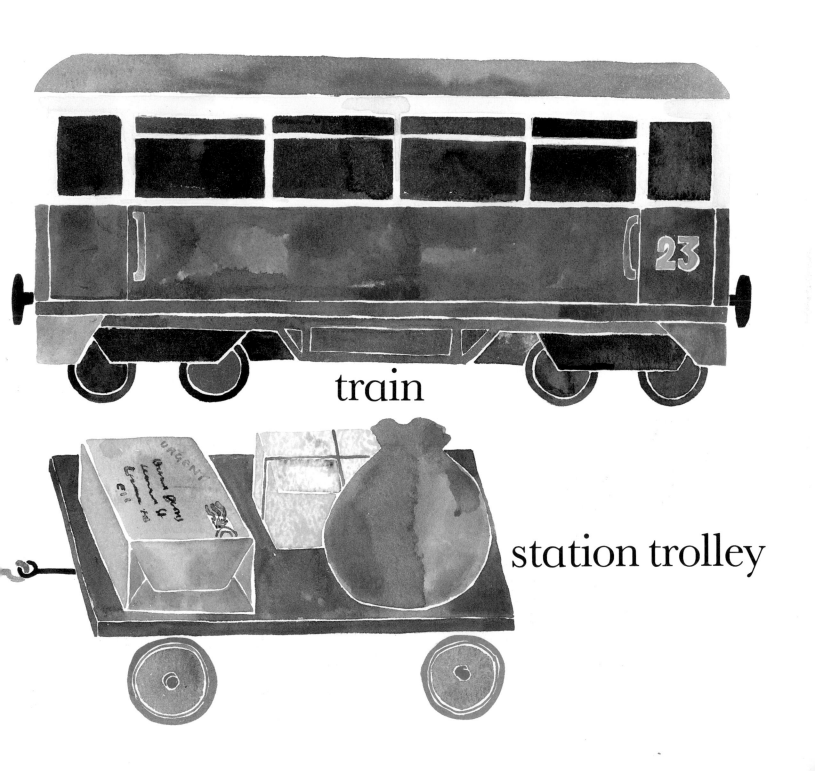

train

station trolley

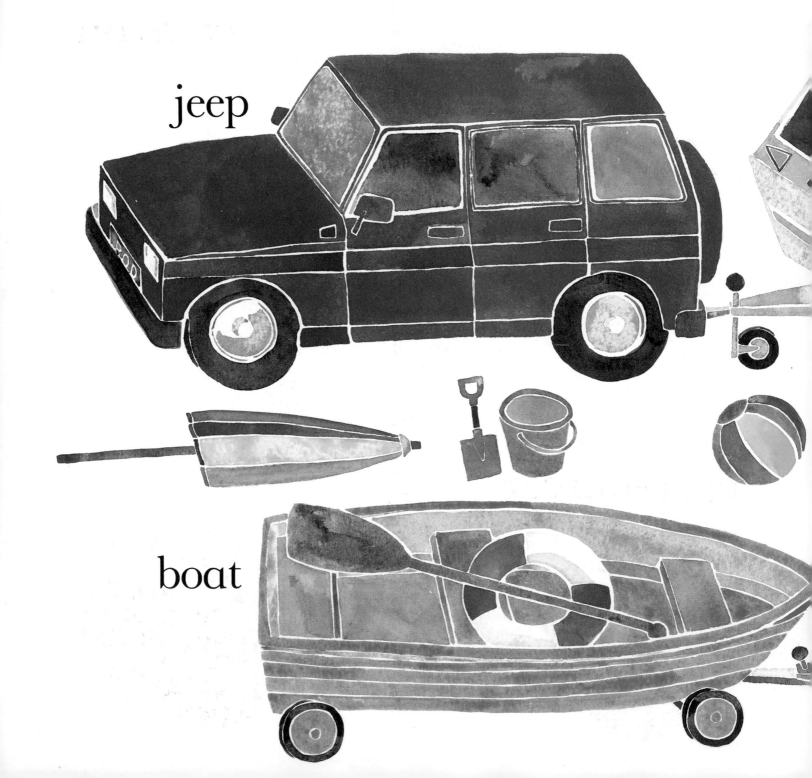

jeep

boat

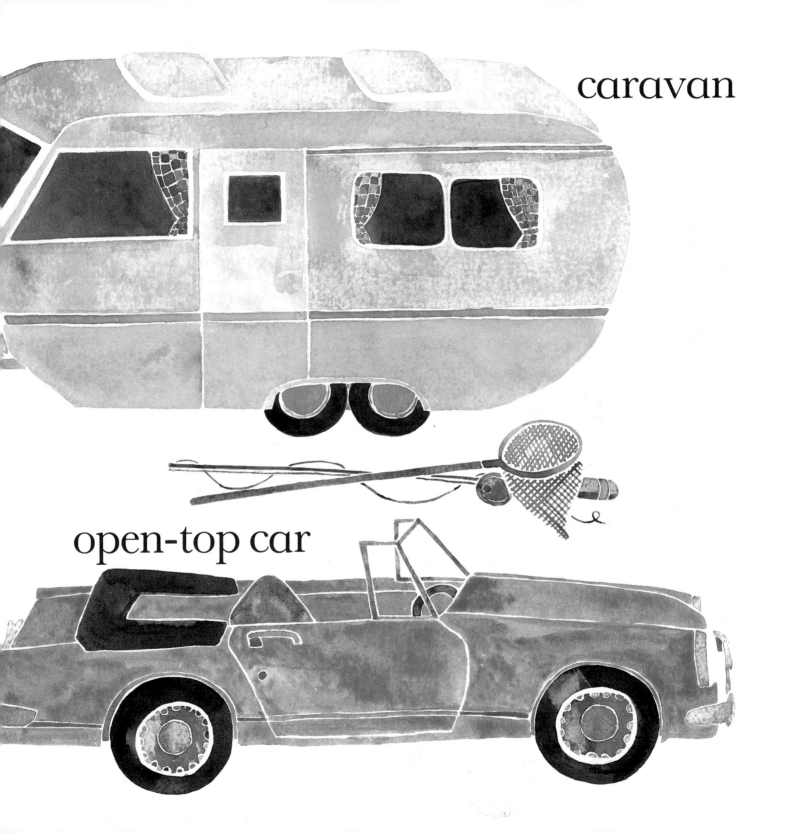

caravan

open-top car

car transporter